Jake

HOUGHTON MIFFLIN   BOSTON

My dog Jake hates
taking trips.

When we leave home,
he yaps and yips.

I pack two bones and
a tennis ball.

But nothing cheers Jake up at all.

It doesn't matter what
we do or see.

There's just one place
Jake wants to be!

6